150 HOT JAZZ LICKS in Tab

By Toby Wine

Cover art by Levin Pfeufer

Recording Credits: Toby Wine, Guitar

Cherry Lane Music Company
Educational Director/Project Supervisor: Susan Poliniak
Director of Publications: Mark Phillips
Publications Coordinator: Rebecca Skidmore

ISBN: 978-1-57560-848-8

Visit our website at www.cherrylaneprint.com

Table of Contents

Introduction

Jazz is not only a musical style but a state of mind. The ability to fly freely over complex chord changes is, paradoxically, the end result of years of preparation and discipline. One must not only learn the repertoire— the melodies, harmonic progressions, and rhythms—but also amass a vast knowledge of scales, modes, and arpeggios to fit each chord type. On top of that are a myriad of schemes and substitutions employed by the style's major practitioners—players whose impact has been so substantial as to render their innovations as pre-requisites for any fledgling jazz musician. What began as a series of simple melodic variations on the pop hits of the early 20th century has evolved into an art form of infinite complexity and choice. So, where do you begin your approach to this often-intimidating musical universe?

It would be presumptuous to suggest this book as your point of entry. There can be no substitute for the long hours required to learn the style's raw materials, nor for the years of attentive listening to the masters, required to familiarize yourself with the attitude, mannerisms, and sense of swing at the heart of the music. Don't look for shortcuts. Do your homework, be patient, and the results will come. Dissect the work of your favorite players, transcribe solos and phrases that appeal to you, and learn the scales and modes that fit the various chords and progressions you find in the standards and jazz classics everybody plays. Go to every open mike and impromptu jam session you can find, and don't be afraid to play with experienced musicians who may kick you around a bit. Those bumps and bruises are all part of the process, a trial by fire that even the great-est players could not (and still don't) avoid.

All that said, this book should give you a little ammunition for the wars. While jazz is essentially an impro-vised music, there is a common vocabulary from which all players can draw, and licks—those phrases and ideas that lie under the fingers and can be applied to common progressions—make up a big part of that vocabulary. Many of these licks have been passed down from generation to generation; they've undergone subtle changes and updates, but have retained their validity and usefulness. Yes, some might call them clichés, but to paraphrase Miles Davis, they don't become clichés without being beautiful and true. As you mature as an improviser, your reliance on these "stock" phrases and clichés will lessen, but until that point, they're a great way to begin to play this wonderful, complex music.

150 Cool Jazz Licks in Tab is a compendium specifically for guitarists. This book gives you ten four-measure licks in each of 15 common categories. The tablature for each illustrates a logical approach to the fingerboard as well as the slides, hammer-ons, and pull-offs one might play to enhance the vocal, expressive nature of the licks themselves. Feel free to alter both the articulations and the fingerings as you see fit—what one player might enjoy or find comfortable may not be to another's liking. I also cannot encourage you enough to take your favorite phrases through all 12 keys in order to have them under your fingers in any situation for which you may want to access them. It's not enough to know a cool lick in C when you find yourself at a jam ses-sion playing tune after tune in E♭ or F.

Before you dive in, here are a few notes on the various categories.

Cmaj7

These licks are mostly built on the major scale (Ionian mode), but also include some Lydian mode sounds, as the raised 11th is a common extension used for major chord soloing. As you'll find in each of the subse-quent categories, chromatic passing tones are sprinkled liberally throughout, as they're the meat and potatoes of the "bebop" linear approach pioneered by Charlie Parker and Dizzy Gillespie, among others. Their stylis-tic innovations remain central to the contemporary jazz vocabulary.

Cm7

These licks include both C Dorian mode and C melodic minor sounds, often in combination. Note that the Dorian mode includes the ♭7th scale degree, resulting in a modal sound, as opposed to the ♮7th found in the melodic minor scale that creates more of a "tonic minor" sound. The minor pentatonic and blues scales also make an appearance. The final licks in this category include some pentatonic cycles in the styles of saxophone icon John Coltrane and pianist McCoy Tyner, in which we take it "out" and get increasingly dissonant before coming to a satisfying resolution.

C7

The dominant chord offers, by far, the most choices to the improviser. The licks here include the Mixolydian mode, blues scales, the "Lydian ♭7" mode (C–D–E–F♯–G–A–B♭), whole tone scales, the "diminished half-whole" scale (C–D♭–E♭–E–G♭–G–A–B♭) and the altered or "Super-Locrian" mode (C–D♭–E♭–E–G♭–A♭–B♭). That's a whole lot of variation in ten short licks! The final phrase includes a mere hint of the many beautiful and complex sounds possible when superimposing triads over different chords— a major technique you'll hear frequently in the work of contemporary jazz guitar masters such as John Scofield, Pat Metheny, and Mike Stern.

Cmaj7–A7–Dm7–G7

I–VII–ii–V is just about the most commonly encountered harmonic sequence in jazz. The licks here show not only how each chord may be approached, but also how to stitch them together into cohesive phrases. Merely learning the right scale for each chord isn't enough if you can't connect them to each other in a musi-cal, satisfying way.

Dm7–G7–Cmaj7–A7

This ultra-common progression is essentially the same as that discussed above, but it begins with the ii chord here rather than the I. Take note of how tension is built by attaching extensions and alterations to the dom-inant chords that are resolved pleasingly in the subsequent measure.

Cmaj7–A7–Dm7–G7–Em7–A7–Dm7–G7

Once again, this chord sequence is a close relative of the previous two, but the chords here go by twice as fast, demanding quicker shifts of scales and modes within each measure. The iii chord is often a stand-in for the I in jazz, with the soloist left to choose whether to approach it as an Em7 or Cmaj7 in the key of C, as shown here. Note that this sequence is the first four measures of "rhythm changes," which is the basis for dozens of tunes in the jazz cannon and is the second most common song structure in the style after the 12-bar blues. While "rhythm changes" are most commonly played in the key of B♭, they can be found in the keys of C, E♭, F, and others as well.

Dm7♭5–G7–Cm

The minor ii–V–i is found in nearly every minor-keyed song in jazz. The C harmonic minor scale is employed frequently here, but it's common to find players layering F minor sounds over a Dm7♭5 chord and using the altered scale (G–A♭–B♭–B–D♭–E♭–F) to build tension over the G7 chord. The tonic minor chord is fre-quently addressed with a melodic minor scale.

C7–F7–C7–Gm7–C7

The first four measures of a jazz blues is usually played with the so-called "fast four," a quick visit to the IV chord in measure 2 before a return to I that builds tension for the "real" trip to IV in measure 5. Notice how tension is built with altered tones in measure 1, which is then resolved in measure 2, setting up the IV chord as a temporary tonic. The same thing happens in measure 4 as you prepare to move back to F7.

Cmaj7–D7

Here we have the first four measures of a very familiar jazz standard (hint: it has something to do with travel by rail). This progression illustrates the approach to the II7 chord, which is most commonly followed by the ii chord. Notice how the II7 is often prefaced by A7 sounds. While not strictly part of the progression, this is a common technique that sets up the targeted chord by building tension immediately preceding its arrival.

Cmaj7–E♭°7–Dm7–G7

This subtle variation on the I–vi–ii–V is found in many of the older standards and "Tin Pan Alley" classics in the repertoire. Essentially, the E♭°7 chord serves as a substitute for D7♭9 (the IIV chord), as the pitches in both are nearly identical (E♭–G♭–A–C for the E♭ chord, and D–F♯–A–C for the D chord).

F♯m7♭5–B7–Em7♭5–A7–Dm7♭5–G7–Cmaj7

This sequence of minor "ii–V's" begins on the ♭5th of the key and resolves to I major; it can be found in a handful of classics from the bebop era. It's also a commonly employed progression for intros and endings. The series of quick key changes and resolutions will put your melodic skills to the test.

Fmaj7–Em7–A7–Dm7–G7–Cm7–F7

This sequence is found in a number of standards and also serves as the first four measures of what's commonly referred to as the "Bird blues," Charlie Parker's substitute progression for the blues in F. You begin on the I chord, then take ii–V down first to the vi (Dm7), and then head on over to the v (Cm7). The ultimate destination here is usually B♭maj7 (IV). This illustrates the clever ways in which jazz musicians devise harmonic labyrinths to travel through between point A and point B in a song. Sure, they could stay on F for four measures and then move to B♭ in measure 5, but what fun would that be?

Fm7–B♭m7–E♭7–A♭maj7

A vi–ii–V–I sequence in A♭, this progression can be found in a number of exceedingly popular jazz standards, including a warhorse of an old show tune and one of Frank Sinatra's most beloved hits. Note the increasingly dissonant nature of the licks as you work through them. Each chord may serve not only its actual harmonic function, but it also may be altered to become the dominant chord that precedes each subsequent harmony. Fm7 may become F7, creating a cadence to B♭m7, which then becomes B♭7 and resolves to E♭7, and so on.

B♭maj7–E♭7–A♭7–G7

This progression occurs in a handful of standards and illustrates one of the many ways in which to get from I to VI7. As in the progression above, each chord can be transformed into a dominant sound to build tension that is resolved on the next chord occurring in the sequence. Thus, B♭maj7 becomes B♭7 and resolves to E♭7, and so on, until you reach your destination at G7.

Bmaj7–D7–Gmaj7–B♭7–E♭maj7–Am7–D7

This final progression is taken from one of saxophonist John Coltrane's most famous songs—it's often used as a proving ground for improvisers because of its incredibly difficult harmonic density. With key changes every two beats, this one presents a never-ending set of challenges, with an equally vast array of solutions possible for this harmonic riddle. With keys moving up in major thirds (B to E♭ to G), you'll have to think fast and navigate the fingerboard with savvy and skill. Good luck, and let's get playing!

About the Author

Toby Wine is a native New Yorker and a freelance guitarist, composer, arranger, and educator. He is a graduate of the Manhattan School of Music, where he studied composition with Manny Albam and Edward Green. Toby has performed with Philip Harper (formerly of the Jazz Messengers), Bob Mover, Ari Ambrose, Joe Shepley, Michael and Carolyn Leonhart (both of Steely Dan), Peter Hartmann, Ian Hendrickson Smith, and the New York–based R&B/Salsa collective Melee, among others. His arrangements and compositions can be heard on recordings by Phillip Harper (*Soulful Sin, The Thirteenth Moon*, Muse Records), Ari Ambrose (*Early Song*, Steeplechase), and Ian Hendrickson Smith (*Up In Smoke*, Sharp Nine). Toby leads his own trio and septet, does studio sessions, and works as a sideman with a variety of tri-state area bandleaders. He spent four years as the music librarian for the Carnegie Hall Jazz band and has performed orchestration and score preparation duties for jazz legend Ornette Coleman. He is the author of numerous Cherry Lane publications, including *1001 Blues Licks, The Art of Texas Blues, 150 Cool Blues Licks in Tab, Steely Dan Legendary Licks,* and *Metallica Under the Microscope.*

Acknowledgments

Many thanks are due to Cherry Lane's head honcho, John Stix, and to my friend and editor, Susan Poliniak, for her insight, guidance, and absurdly patient good nature. Additional thanks to the extended Cherry Lane family for all that they do so well. Thanks as well to my parents, Rosemary and Jerry, and to Lissette, Bibi, Bob, Jack, Noah, Enid, Mover, Humph (R.I.P.), and all of the great teachers I've ever had.

TRACK 01

Note: Track 1 contains tuning pitches.

Cmaj7

TRACK 02

Cmaj7

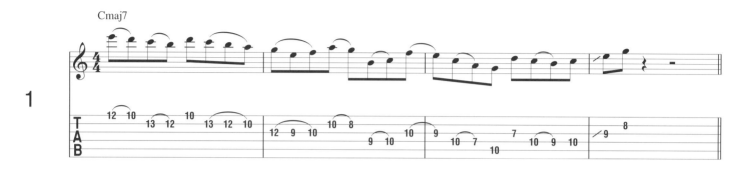

1

TRACK 02

Cmaj7

2

TRACK 03

Cmaj7

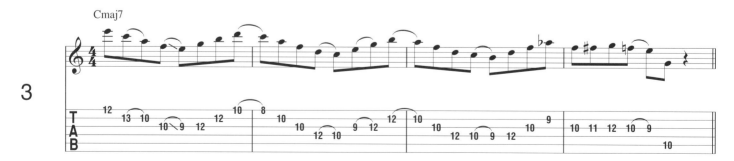

3

4

Cmaj7

5

Cmaj7

6

Cmaj7

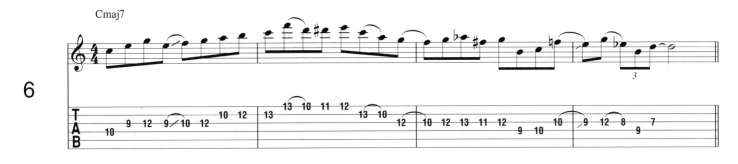

7

Cmaj7

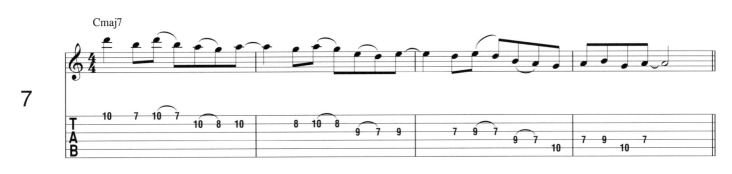

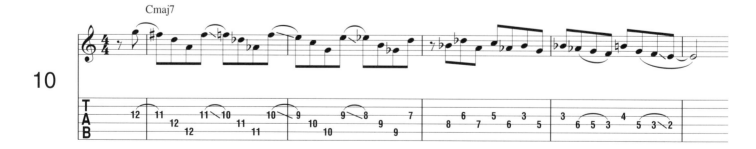

Cm7

TRACK 07

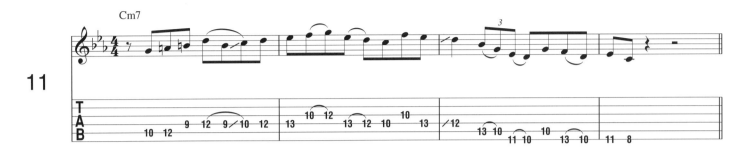

11

TRACK 07

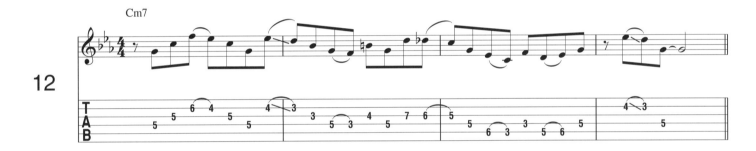

12

TRACK 08

13

TRACK 08

14

TRACK 09

15

TRACK 09

16

TRACK 10

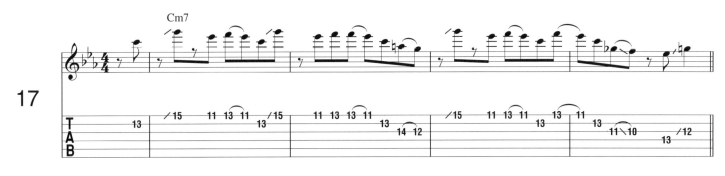

17

TRACK 10

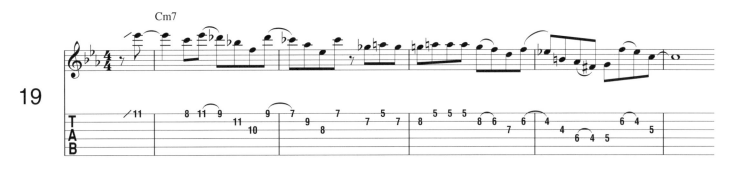

18

TRACK 11

19

TRACK 11

20

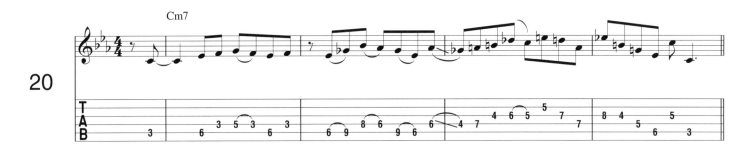

C7

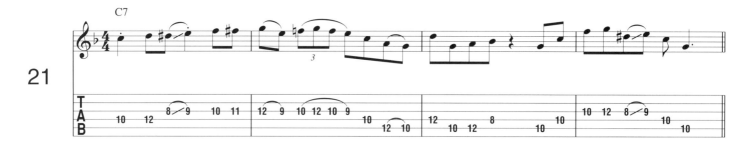

21

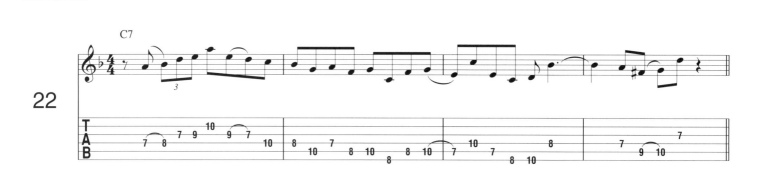

22

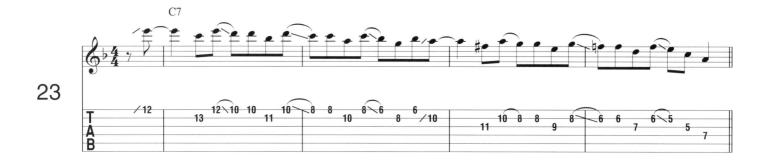

23

24

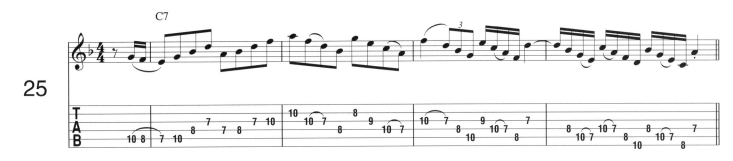

25

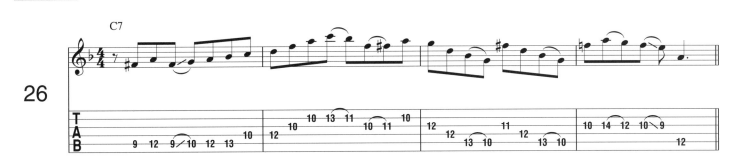

26

27

TRACK 15

28

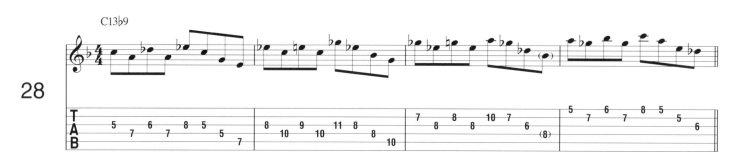

TRACK 16

29

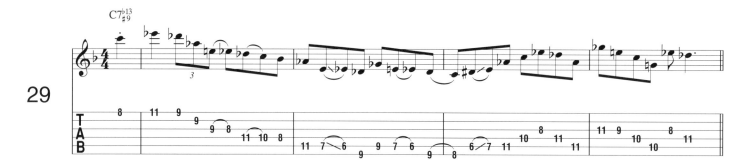

TRACK 16

30

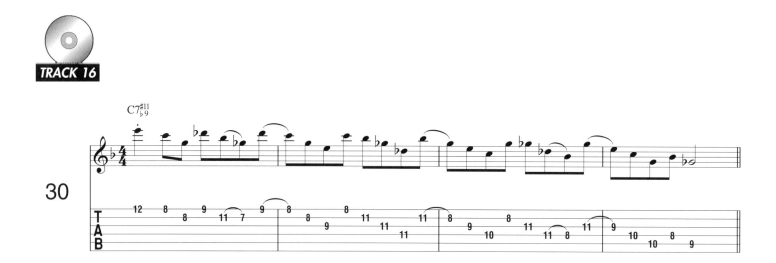

Cmaj7–A7–Dm7–G7

31

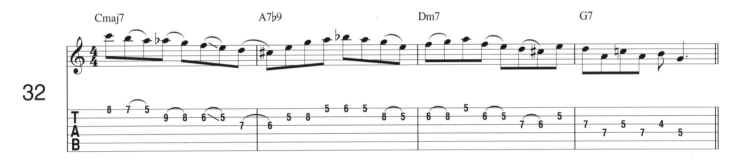

32

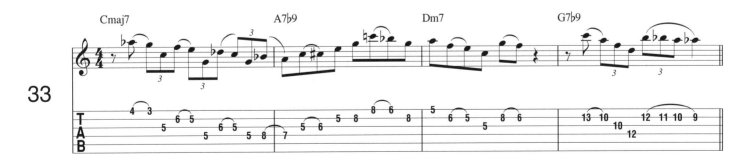

33

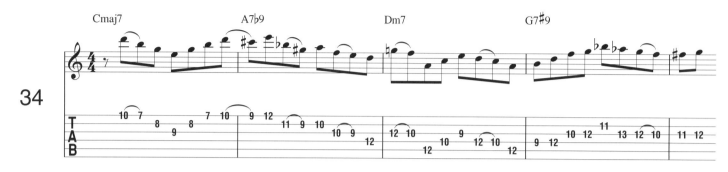

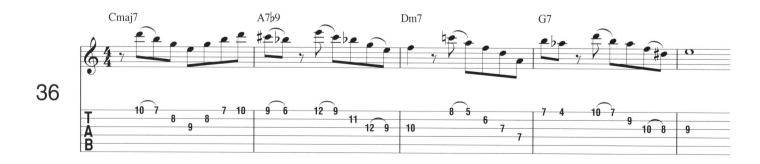

TRACK 20

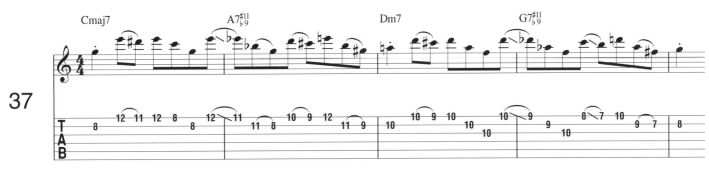

37

TRACK 20

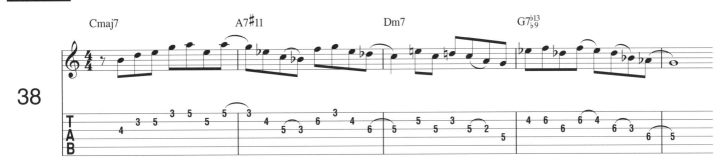

38

TRACK 21

39

TRACK 21

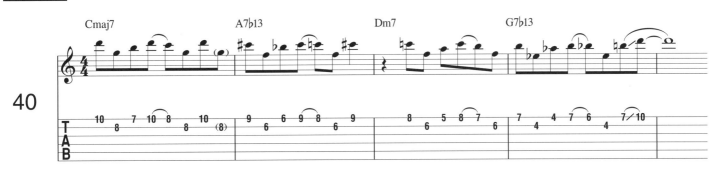

40

Dm7–G7–Cmaj7–A7

TRACK 22

TRACK 22

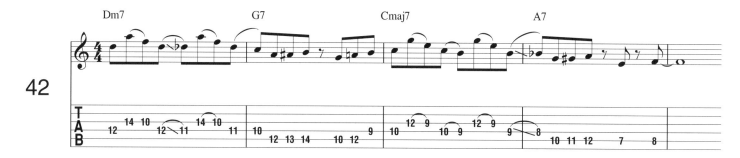

TRACK 23

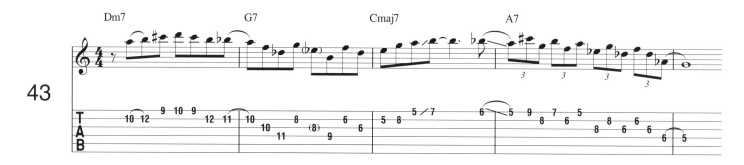

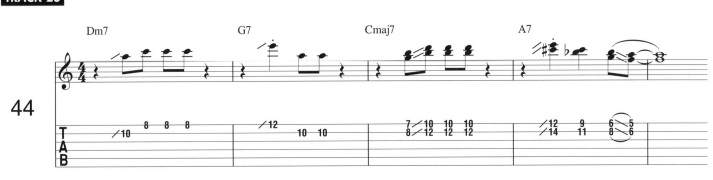

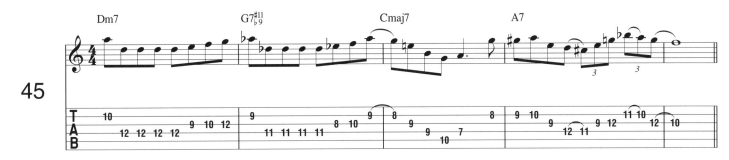

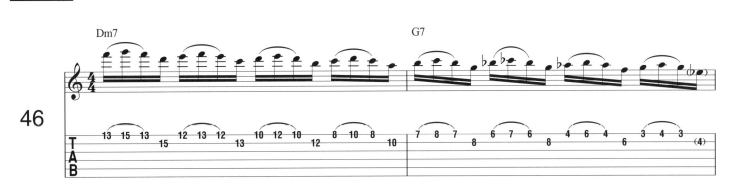

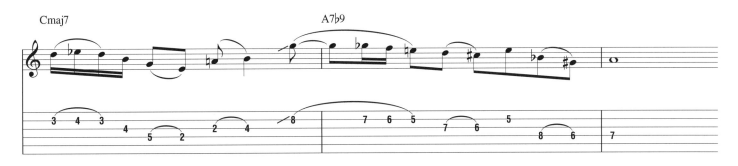

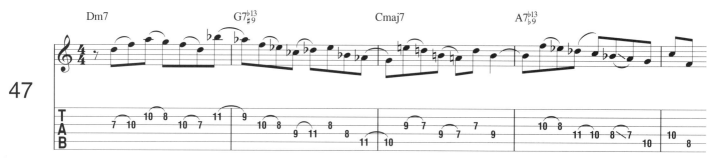

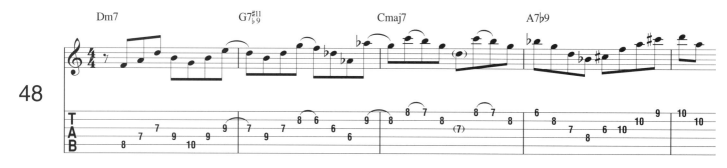

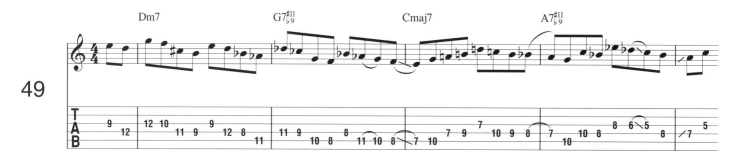

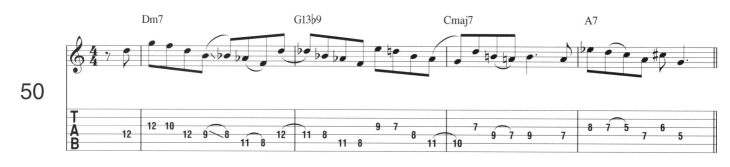

Cmaj7–A7–Dm7–G7–Em7–A7–Dm7–G7

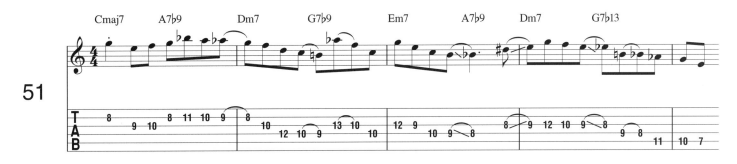

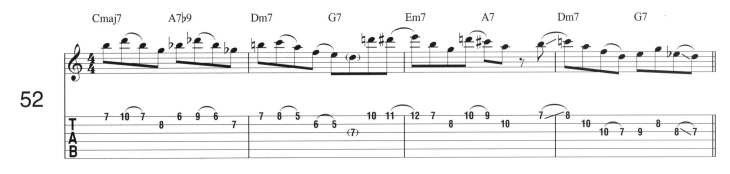

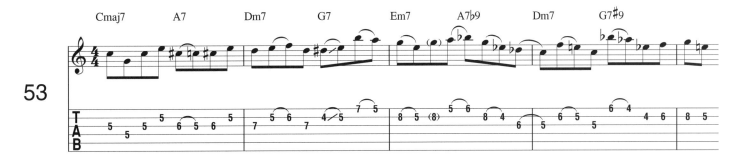

TRACK 28

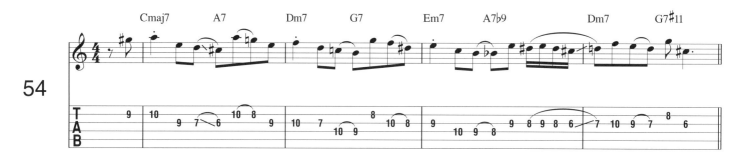

TRACK 29

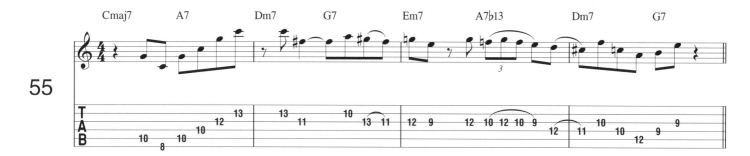

TRACK 29

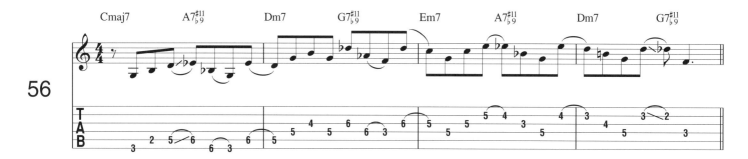

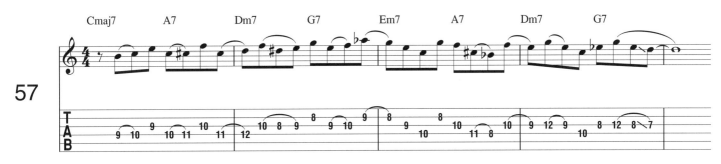

57

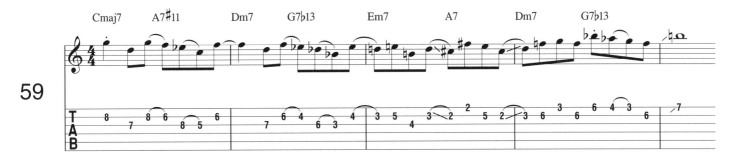

58

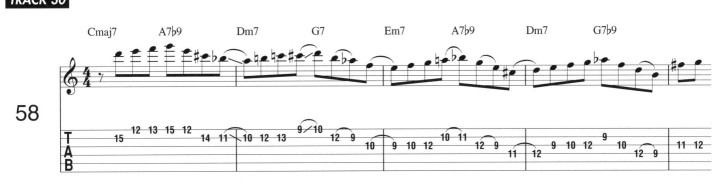

59

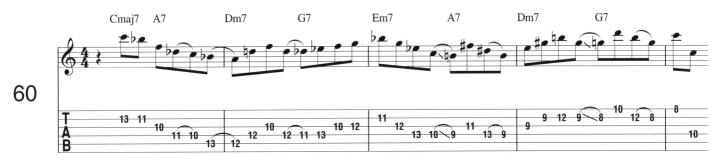

60

Dm7♭5–G7–Cm

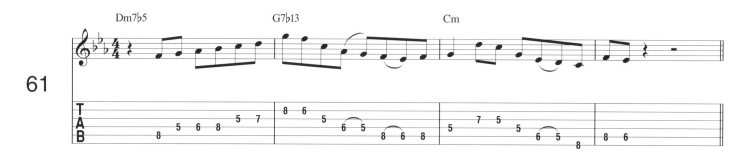

61

TRACK 32

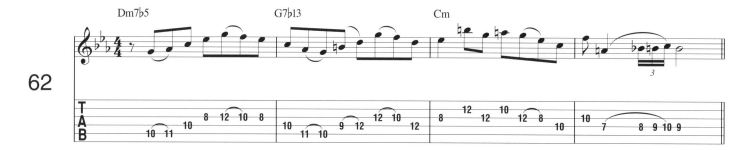

62

TRACK 33

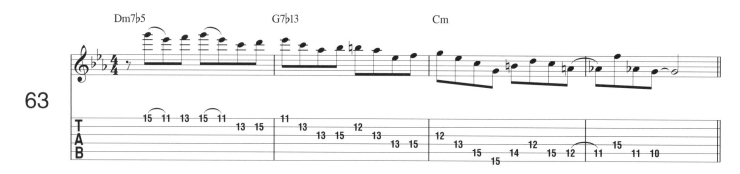

63

TRACK 33

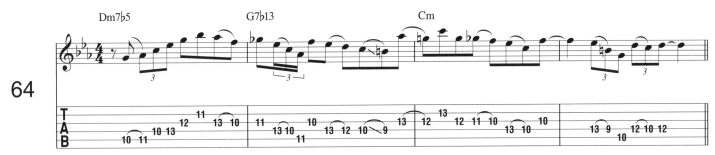

64

TRACK 34

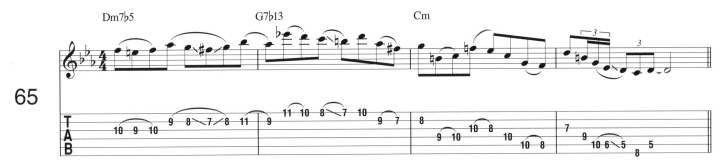

65

TRACK 34

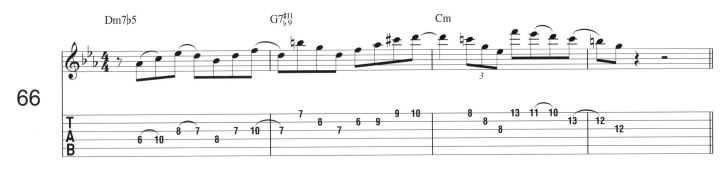

66

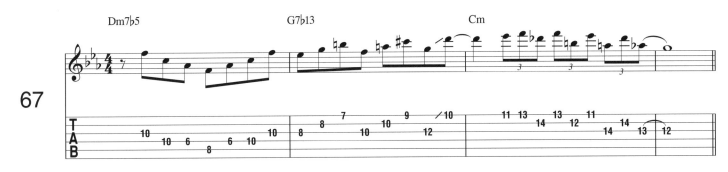

TRACK 35

67

TRACK 35

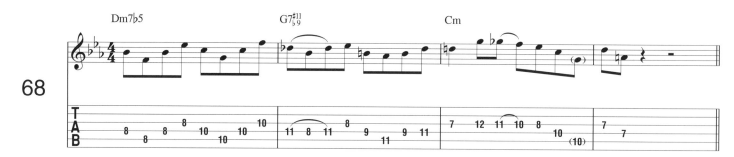

68

TRACK 36

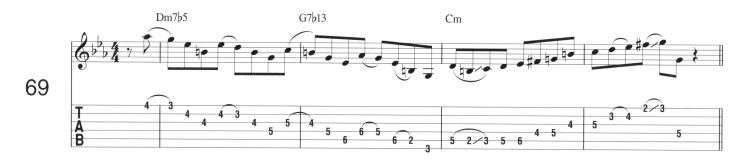

69

TRACK 36

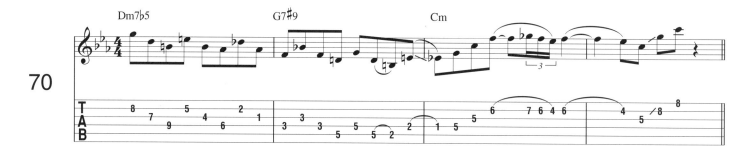

70

C7–F7–C7–Gm7–C7

TRACK 37

71

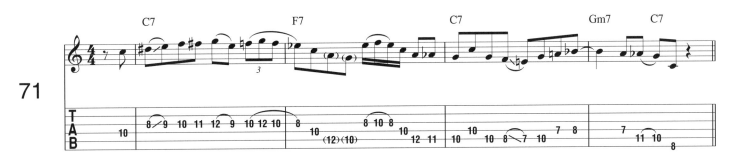

TRACK 37

72

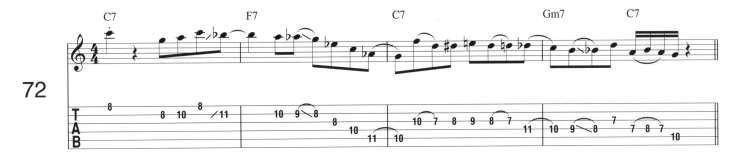

TRACK 38

73

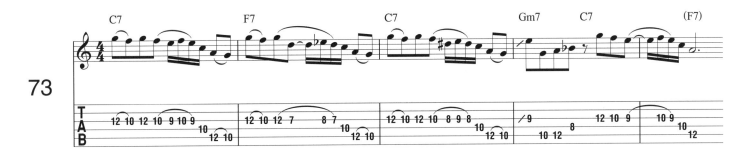

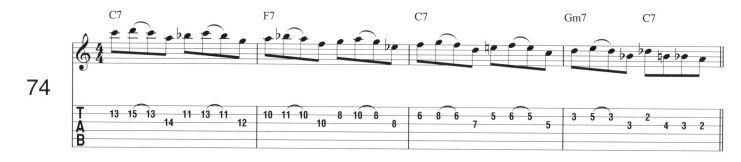

74

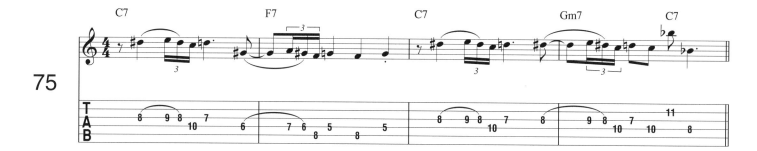

75

TRACK 39

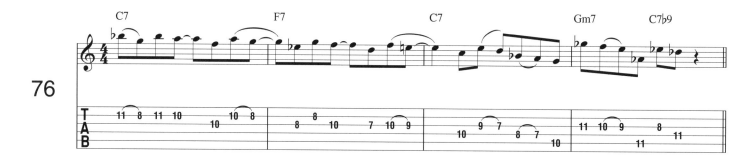

76

TRACK 40

77

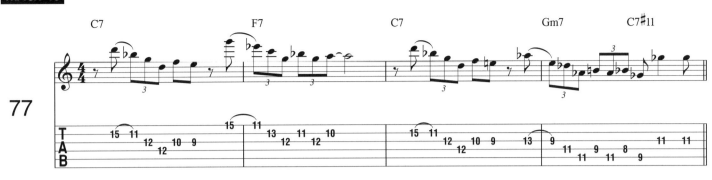

TRACK 40

78

TRACK 41

79

TRACK 41

80

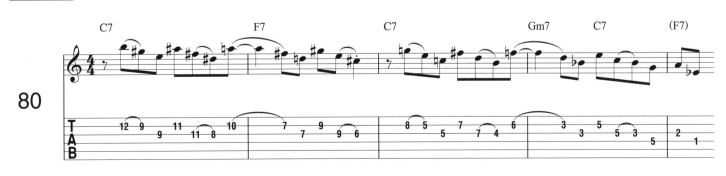

Cmaj7–D7

TRACK 42

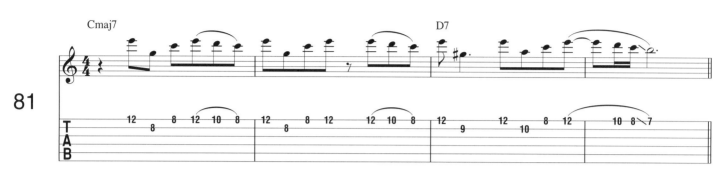

81

TRACK 42

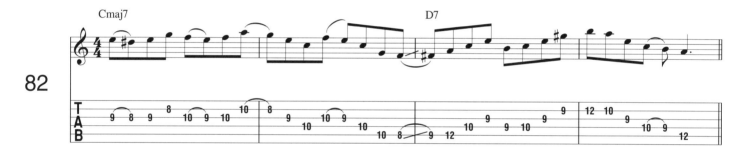

82

TRACK 43

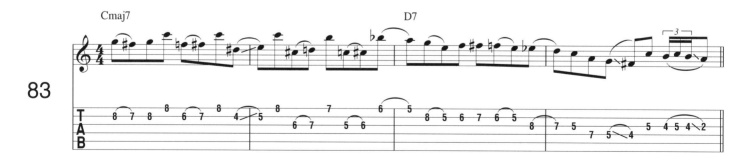

83

TRACK 43

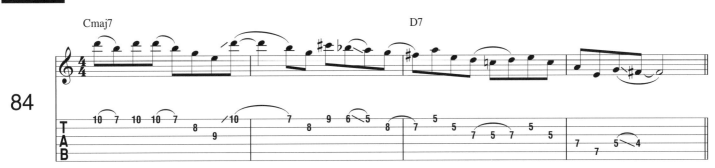

84

TRACK 44

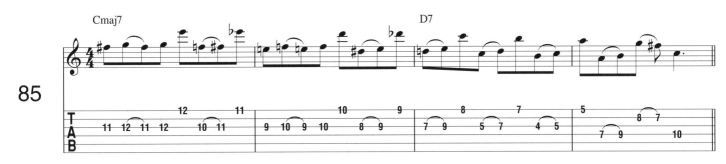

85

TRACK 44

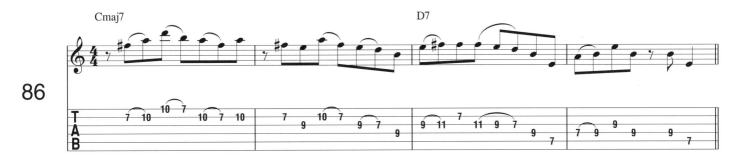

86

TRACK 45

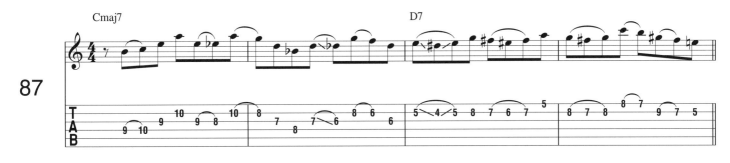

87

TRACK 45

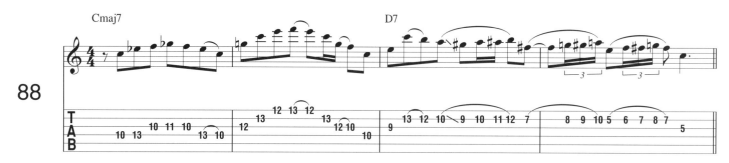

88

TRACK 46

89

TRACK 46

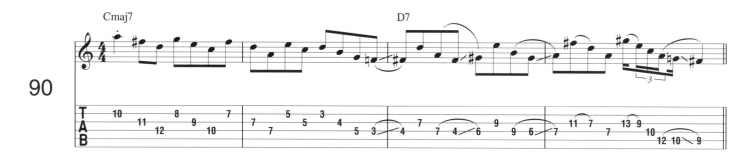

90

Cmaj7–E♭°7–Dm7–G7

91

92

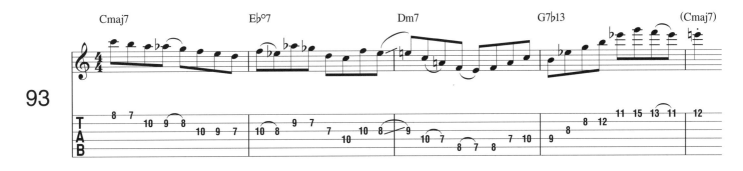

93

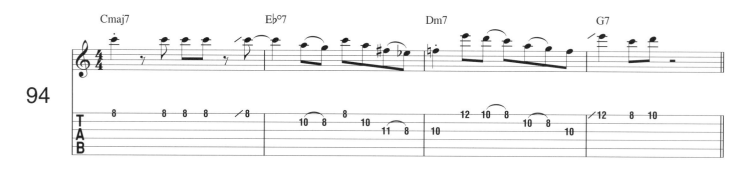

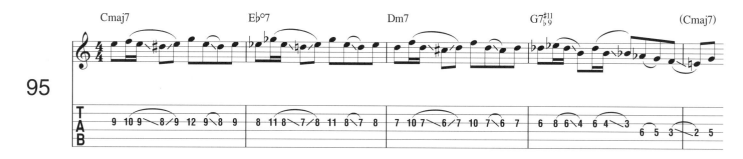

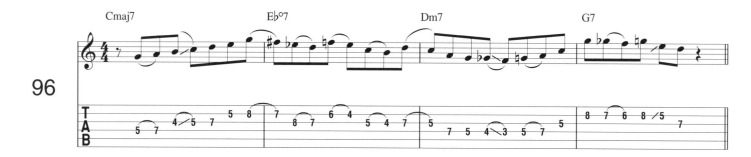

97

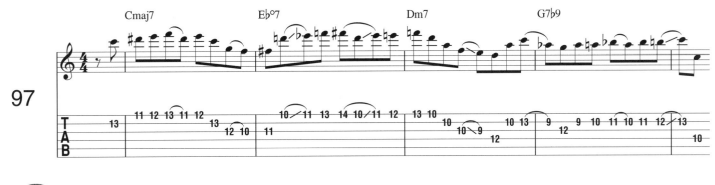

98

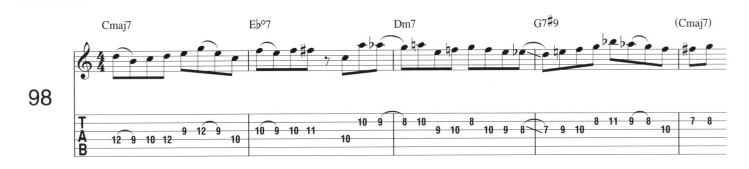

99

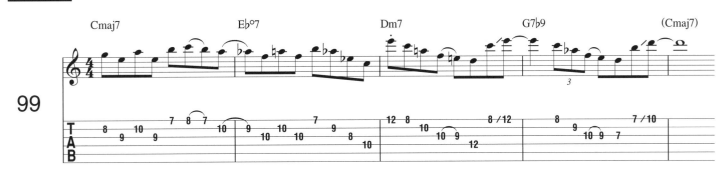

100

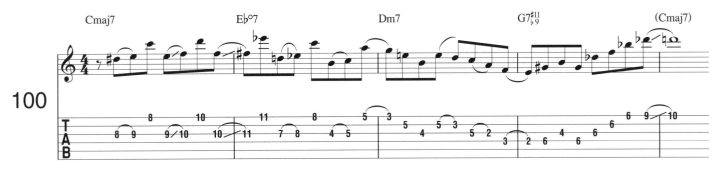

F#m7♭5–B7–Em7♭5–A7–Dm7♭5–G7–Cmaj7

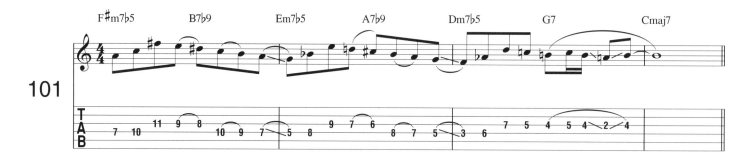

101

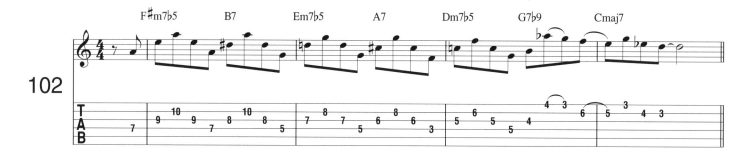

102

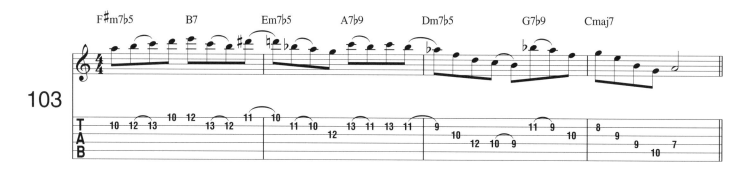

103

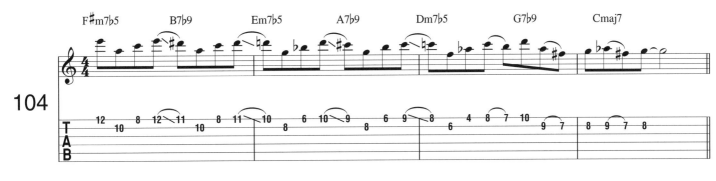

104

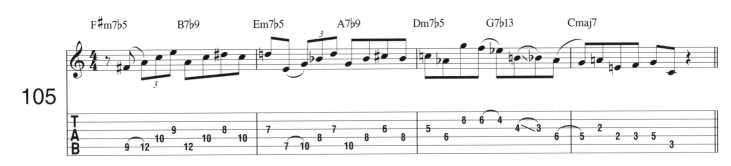

105

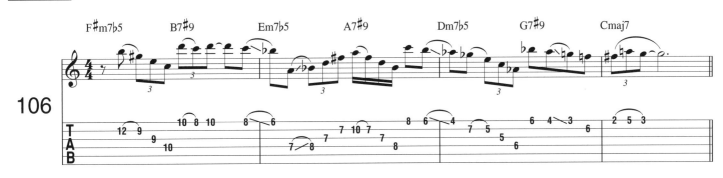

106

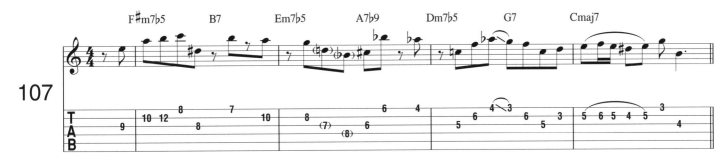

107

TRACK 55

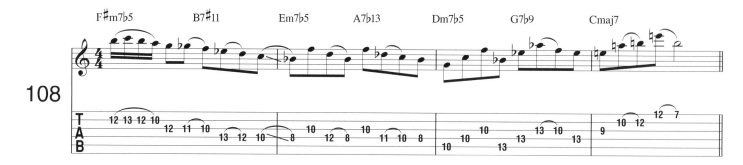

108

TRACK 56

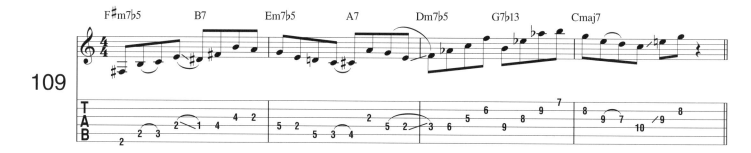

109

TRACK 56

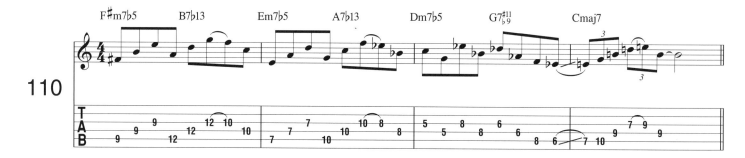

110

Fmaj7–Em7–A7–Dm7–G7–Cm7–F7

TRACK 57

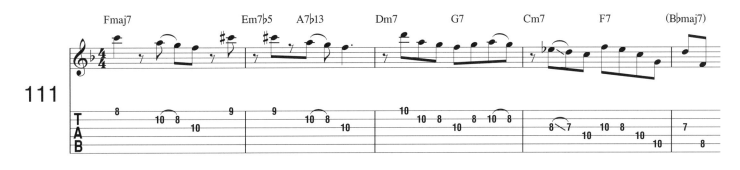

111

TRACK 57

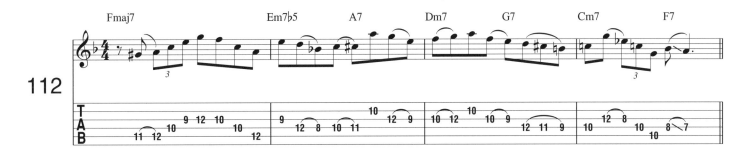

112

TRACK 58

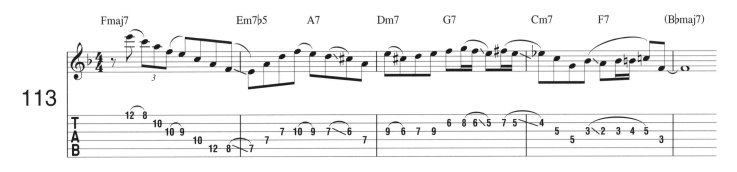

113

Fmaj7–Em7–A7–Dm7–G7–Cm7–F7 *cont.*

TRACK 58

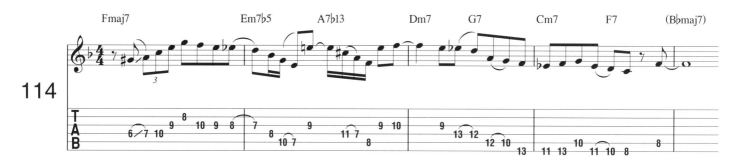

TRACK 59

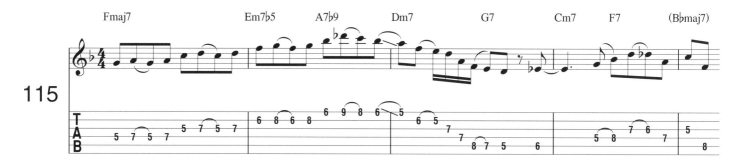

TRACK 59

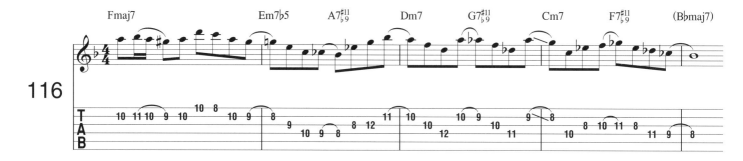

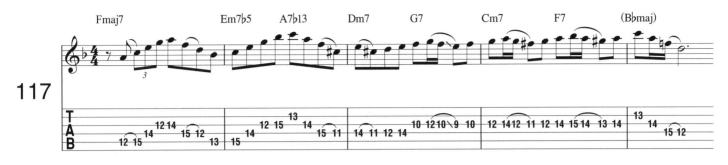

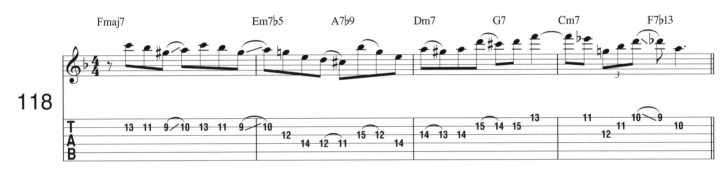

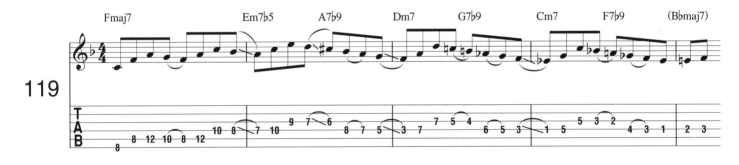

Fm7–B♭m7–E♭7–A♭maj7

TRACK 62

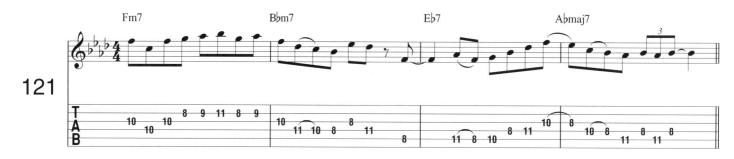

121

TRACK 62

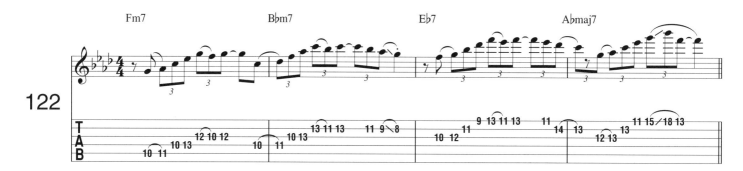

122

TRACK 63

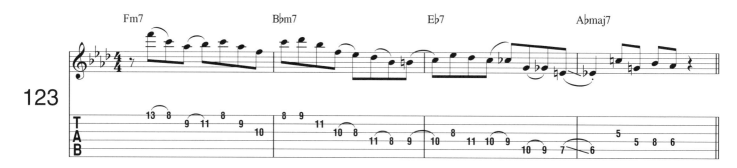

123

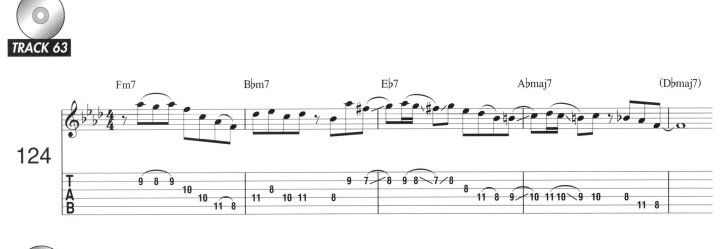

124

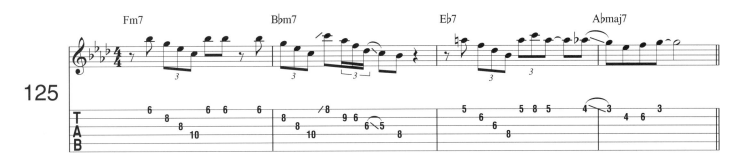

125

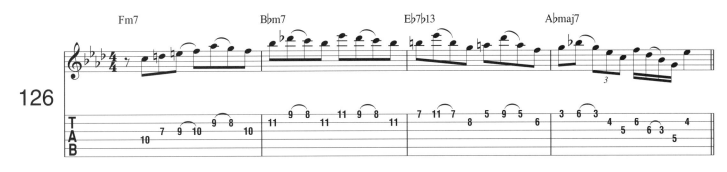

126

127

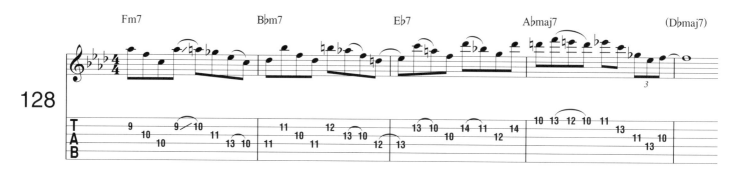

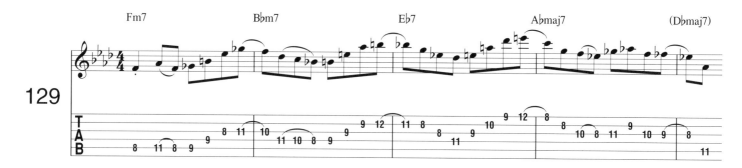

B♭maj7–E♭7–A♭7–G7

TRACK 67

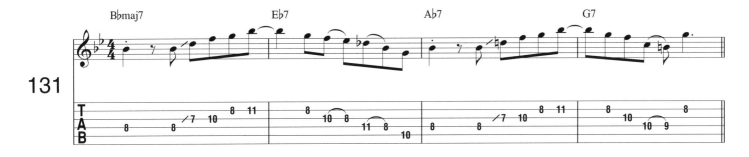

131

TRACK 67

132

TRACK 68

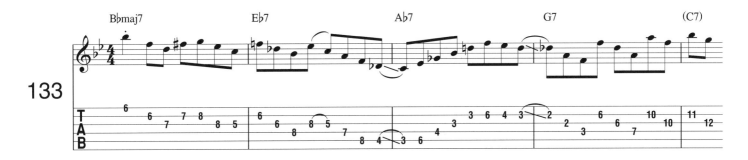

133

TRACK 68

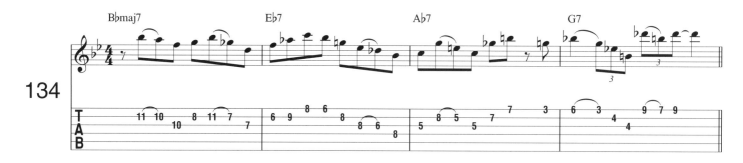

134

TRACK 69

135

TRACK 69

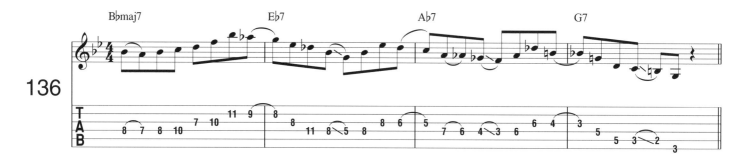

136

137

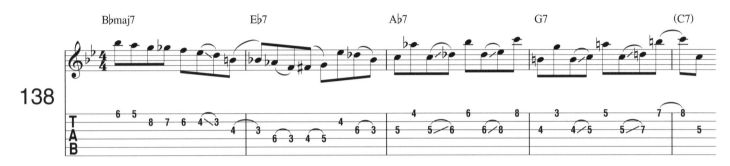

138

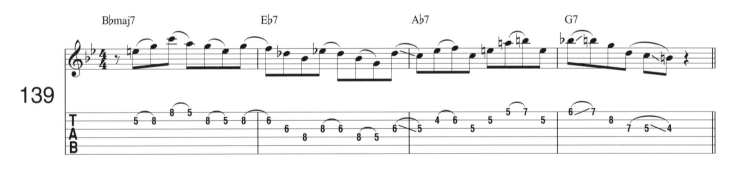

139

140

Bmaj7–D7–Gmaj7–B♭7–E♭maj7–Am7–D7

TRACK 72

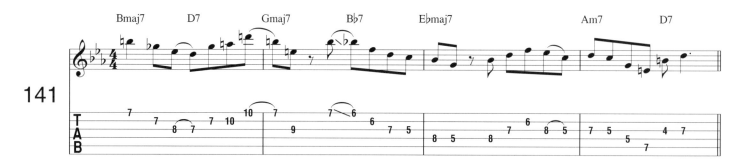

141

TRACK 72

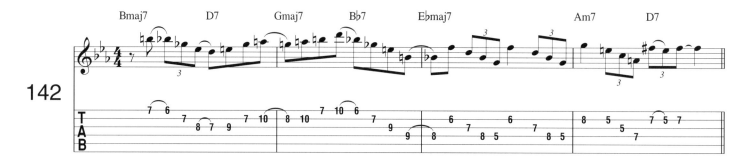

142

TRACK 73

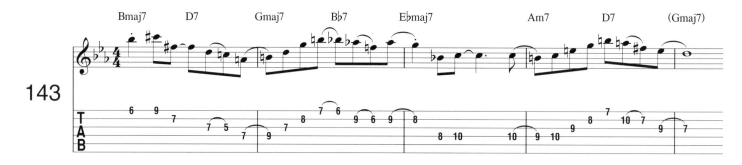

143

TRACK 73

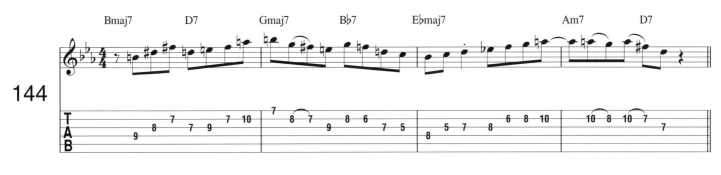

144

TRACK 74

145

TRACK 74

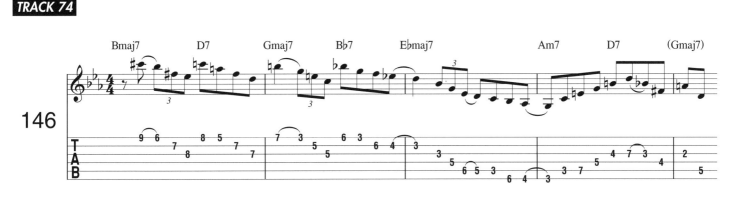

146

TRACK 75

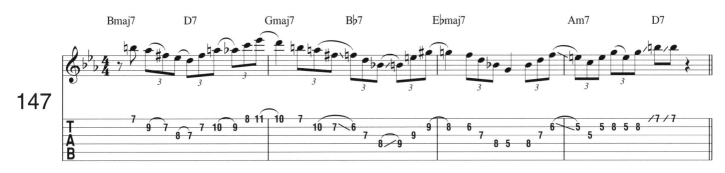

147

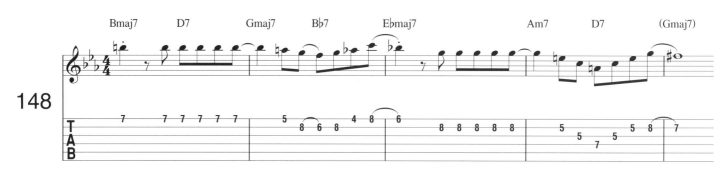

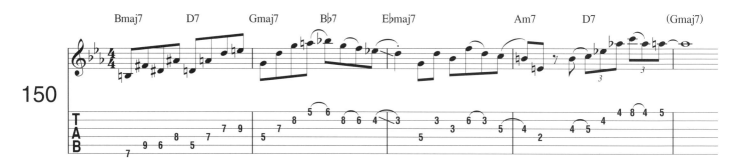